ULTIMATE
GEOMETRIC
COLORING BOOK

ISBN: 9798650188834

This Book
Belongs To

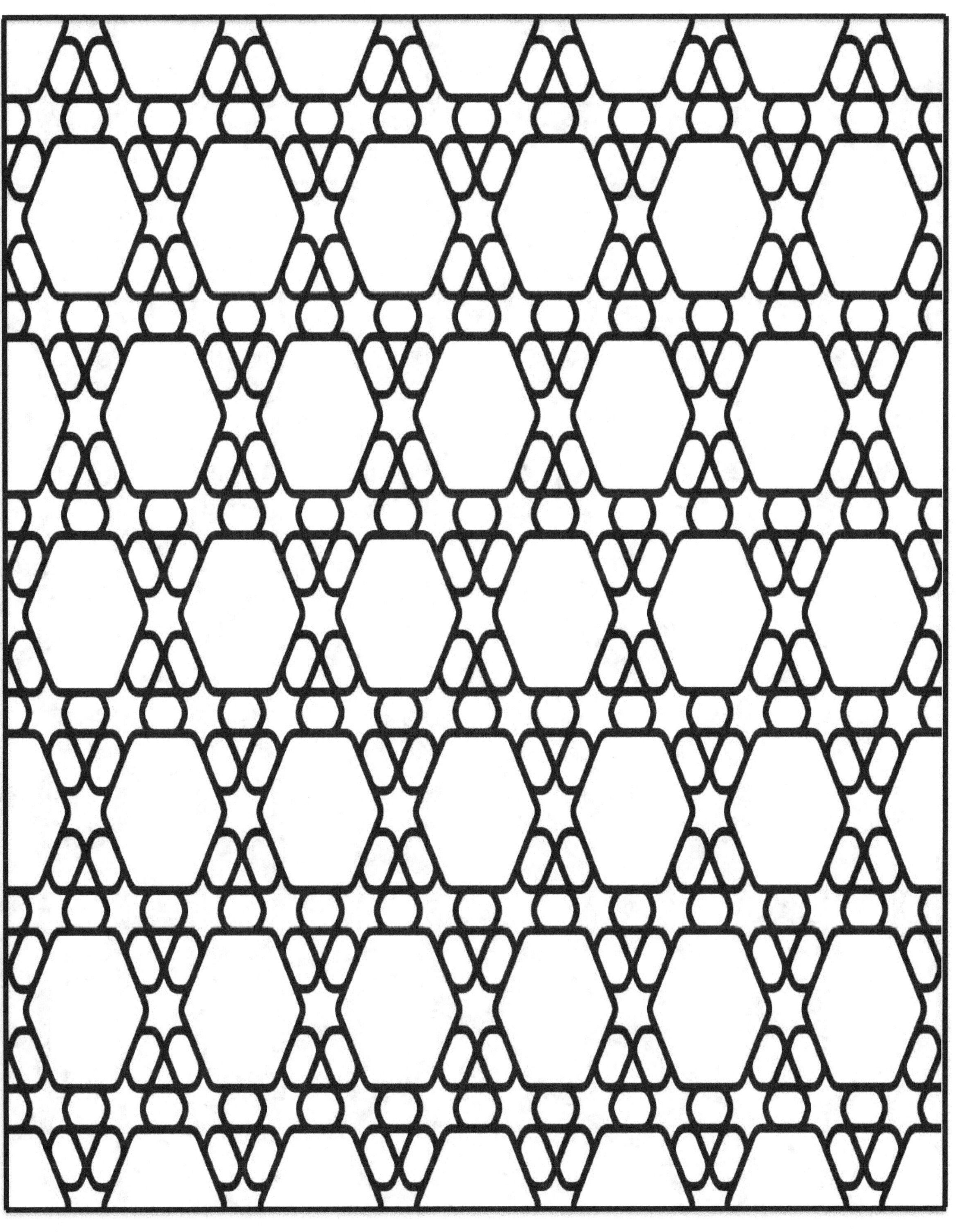

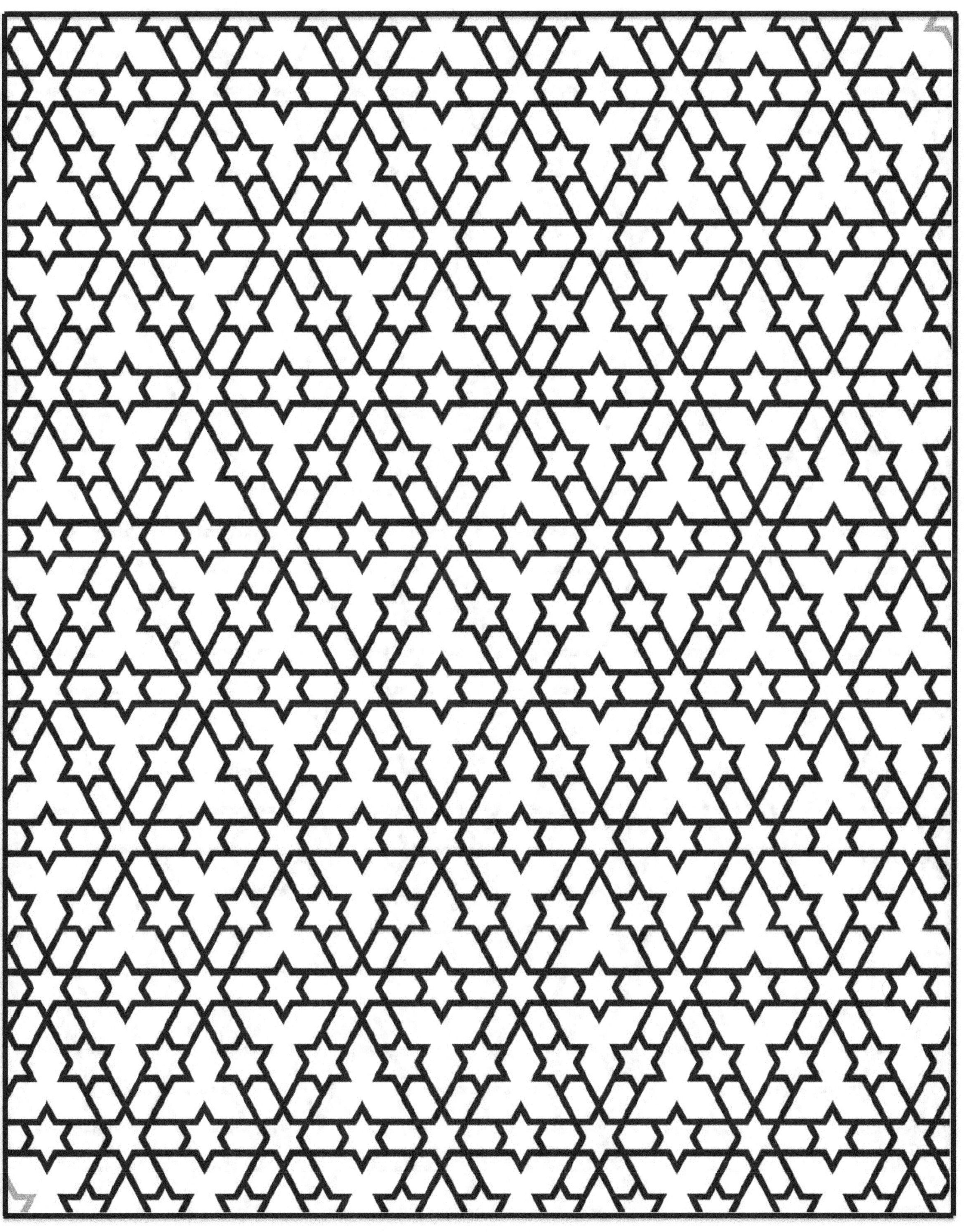

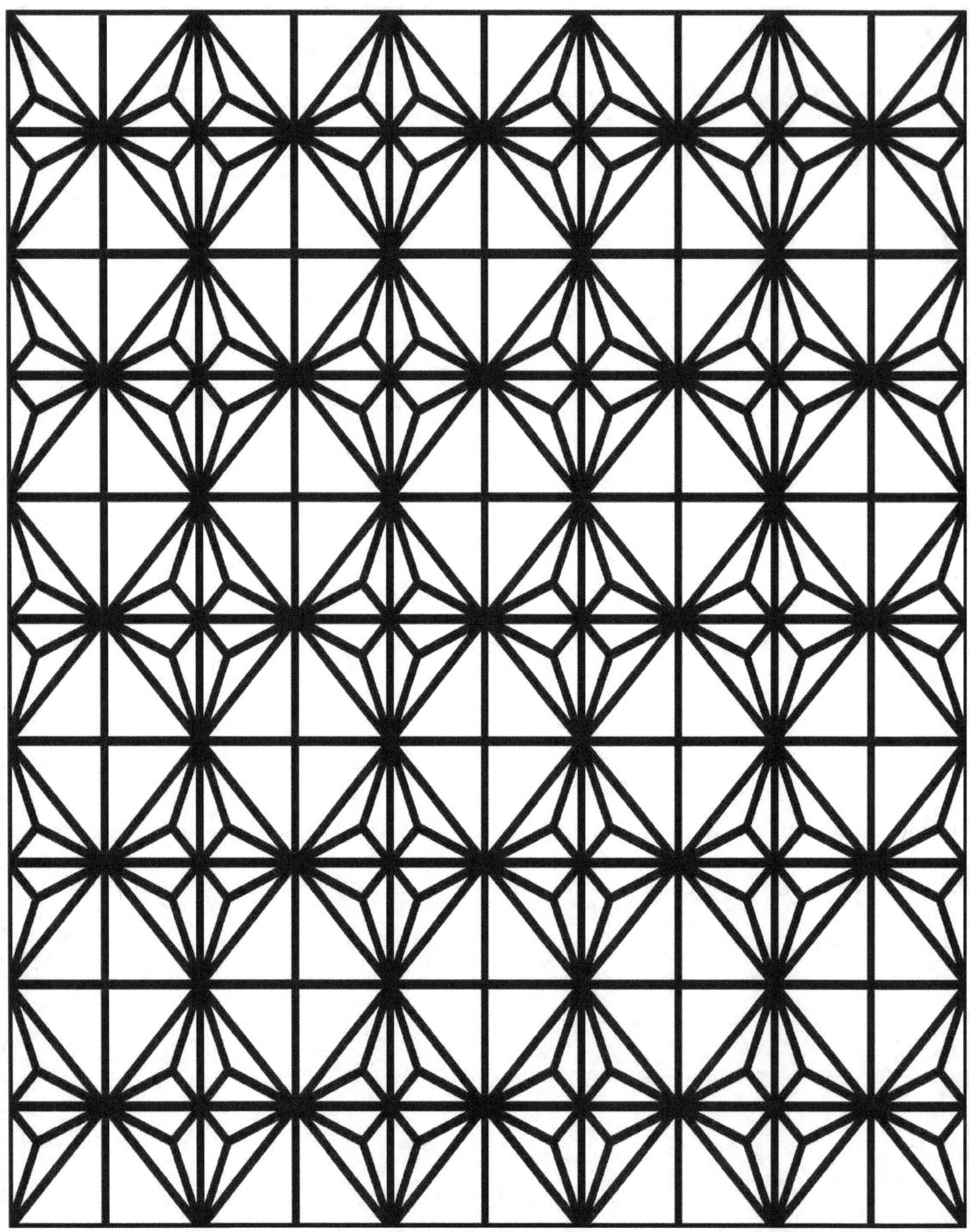

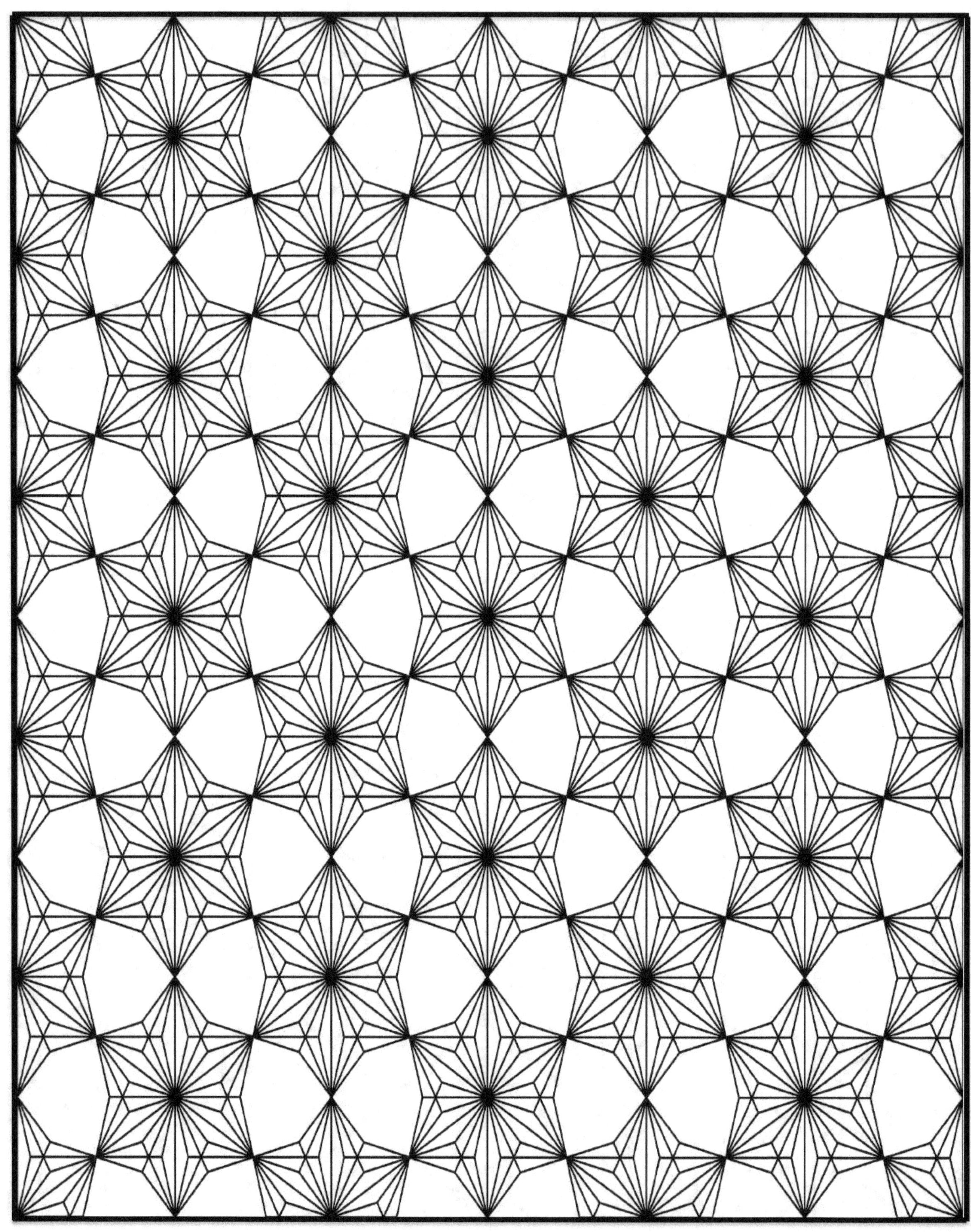

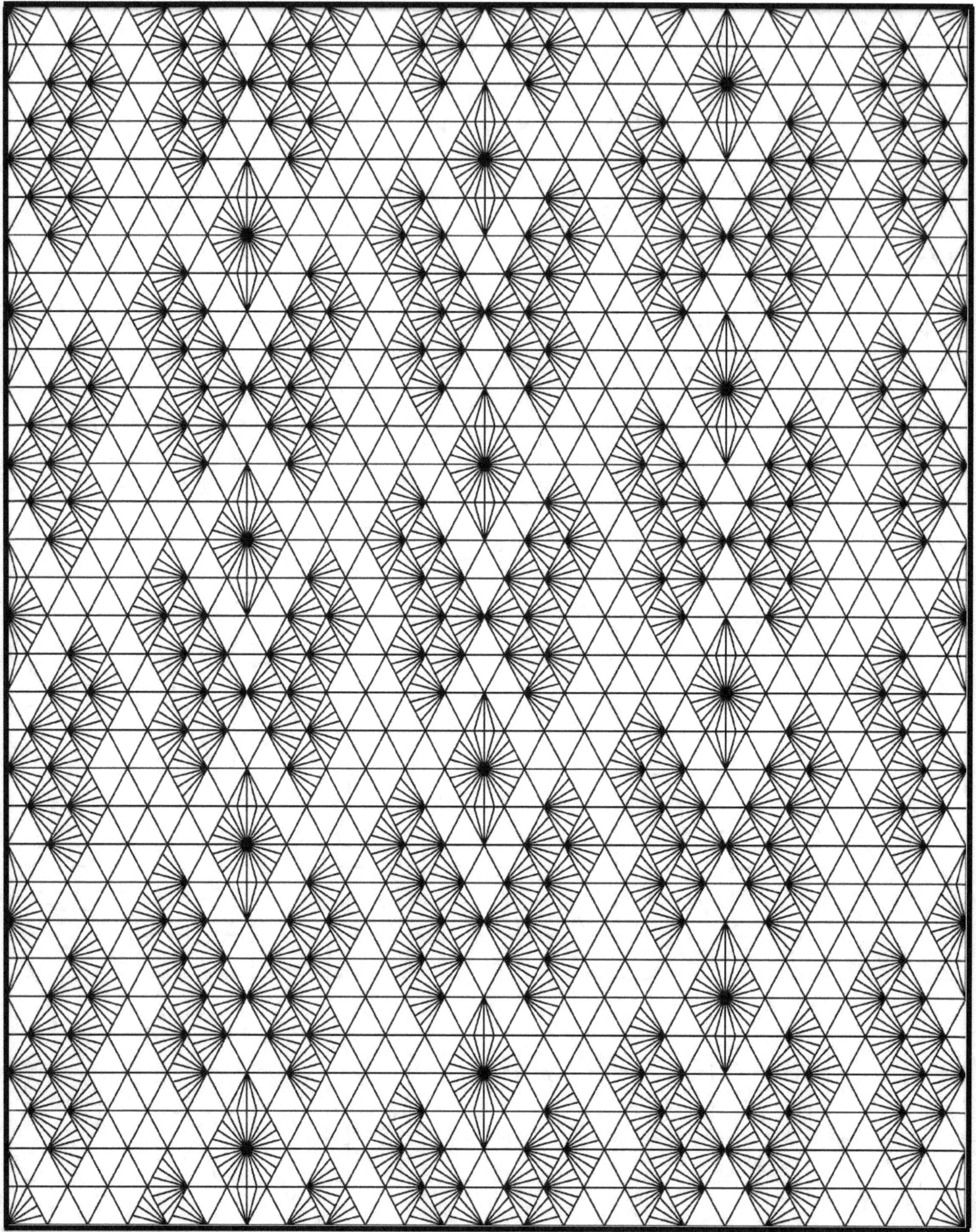

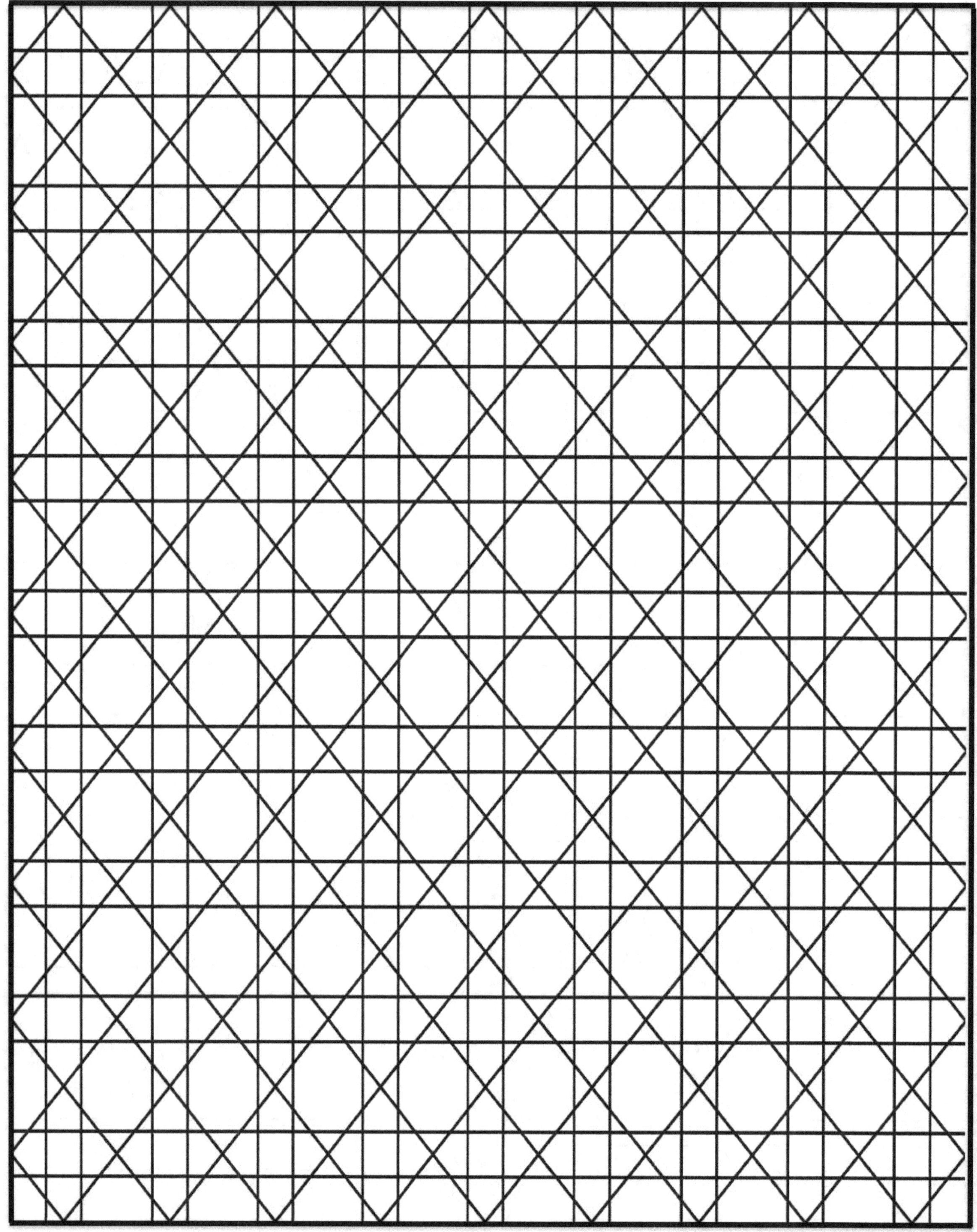

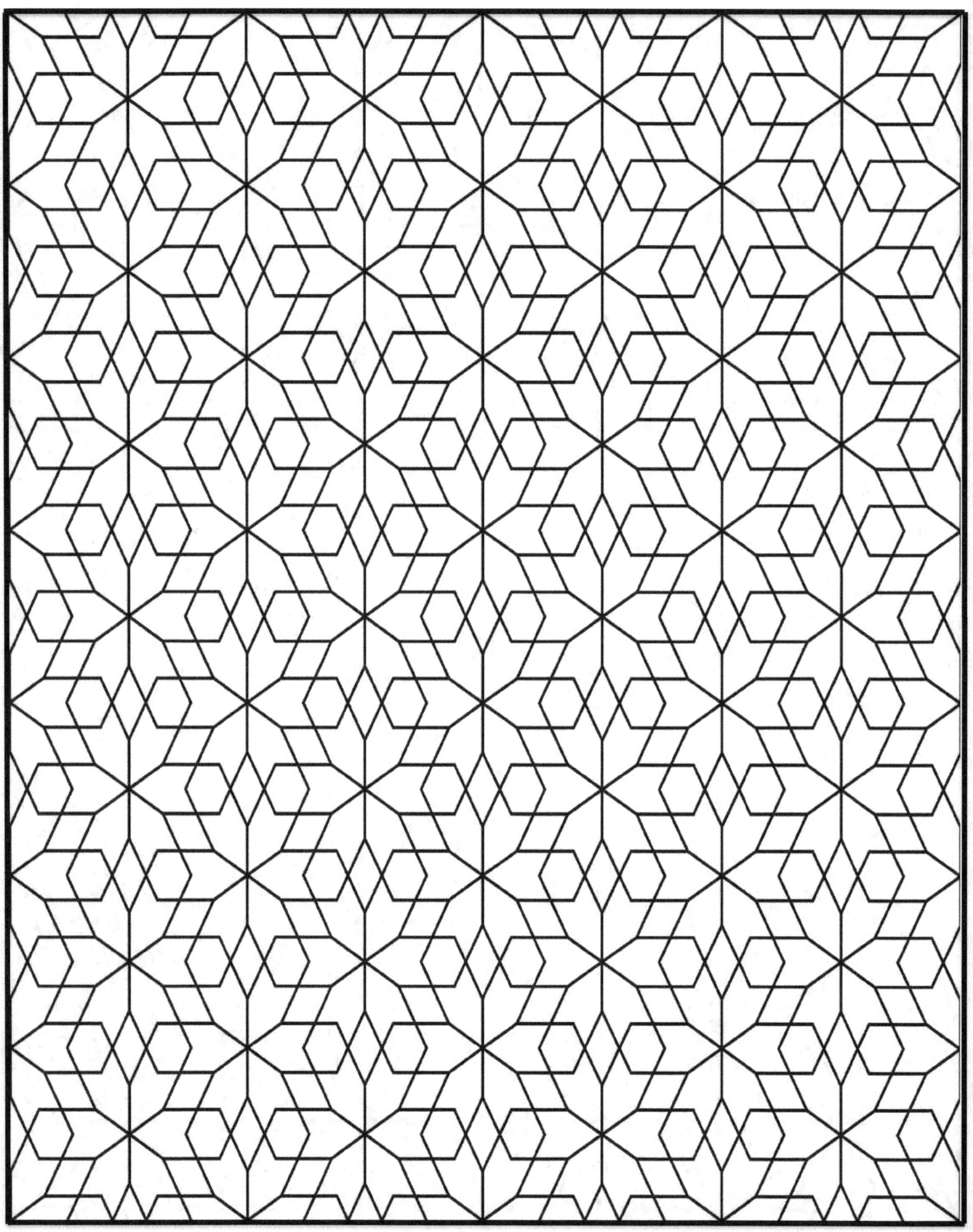